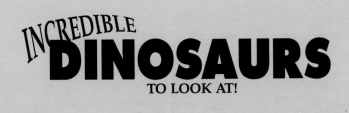

INCREDIBLE DINOSAURS
TO LOOK AT!

This book belongs to:

. . . .

INCREDIBLE DINOSAURS

TO LOOK AT!

The largest of the early
dinosaurs was the
PLATEOSAURUS
(plat'e'o'SORE'us). It
was about 20 feet long,
with a small head and
a whip-like tail. This
swift moving
animal ate
only plants.

The APATOSAURUS (a'pat'o'SORE'us), formerly known as the BRONTOSAURUS (bron'toe'SORE'us), means "deceptive lizard." These plant-eaters stayed together in herds for protection from meat-eating dinosaurs.

ALLOSAURUS
(al'lo'SORE'us)
had strong claws
and deadly teeth.
Although this
meat-eater was
only 35 feet long,
it was capable
of fighting the
Apatosaurus,
which was
twice its size.

The new, smaller dinosaurs moved slowly, but were protected by thick, spiked coats of armor.

The STEGOSAURUS (steg'o'SORE'us) had large, bony plates on its back and a thick tail with sharp spikes. It was 20 feet long, but had a brain the size of a walnut.

The PROTOCERATOPS (pro'toe'SER'o'tops) was about six feet long, ate plants, and was often the target of the large meat-eaters. It could defend itself because it was protected by armor and a tough, bony frill on the back of its head.

The GORGOSAURUS
(gor'go'SORE'us) stood nearly
40 feet tall and was a fierce
meat-eater. Its long, powerful
legs made it a swift, two-legged
runner. Its strong jaw and
dagger-like teeth were used
to grab and eat its food.

The
IGUANODON
(i'GWAN'o'don),
whose name means
"lizard tooth," was
smaller than the
Trachodon, with
human shaped
hands. A spiked
claw formed its
thumb. Balancing
on its webbed feet
and tail, it walked
on two legs.

Some dinosaurs looked like large, fierce rhinoceroses, with horns on their heads. The horns protected these plant-eaters from meat-eating predators.

The STYRACOSAURUS (sty'rack'o'SORE'us) had a crown of six long horns on its head and one uptilted on its nose. It was known as the "spike lizard."

TYRANNOSAURUS
(tie'ran'o'SORE'us)

This ferocious dinosaur, was two stories high and nearly 60 feet long. A savage hunter, it was feared by other dinosaurs because of its powerful jaws and sharp teeth. This "terrible lizard" was one of the last dinosaurs on the planet.

TRICERATOPS (try'SER'a'tops) had a long, bony collar and three sharp horns. It resembled an armored tank. Approximately six feet tall, this eight-ton plant-eater was feared by the larger meat-eaters.

The PTERANODON (ter'AN'o'don), a
large flying reptile, had a wingspread
of over 20 feet. With no teeth, it is
thought to have fed like a pelican,
scooping up fish and swallowing
them whole.

DIMETRODON (di'ME'tra'don), known as "finback," consumed small reptiles. The many blood vessels of its fin carried blood warmed by the sun into other parts of its body. Its name means "two kinds of teeth."

LAMBEOSAURUS
(lam'be'uh'SORE'us)
had two distinct features on its head.
A tall, rectangular, hollow crest
pointed forward from the front of
the head, while a bony, solid spike
emerged from the crown pointing
backward. This member of the duckbill
family moved on
all four legs while
eating vegetation.

PARASAUROLOPHUS
(par'a'SORE'oh'LOAF'us)
had a single, horn-like crest
on the top of its head which
pointed backward. This
dinosaur traveled on all four
legs and ate vegetation.

CORYTHOSAURUS (ko'RITH'oh'SORE'us) is the best known of the duck-billed dinosaurs. It was a large dinosaur, over 33 feet in length, with a high narrow crest at the top of its head.

**Look for other
titles in this series:**

Beautiful Zoo Animals
Friendly Farm Animals
Furry Wild Animals